Sexboml

The Life and Death of Jayne Mansfield

Sexboml

The Life and Death of Jayne Mansfield

Sexbomb

The Life and Death of Jayne Mansfield

by Guus Luijters and Gerard Timmer

Translated from the Dutch by Josh Pachter

Citadel Press
Secaucus, New Jersey

For Jan Cremer

Library of Congress Cataloging-in-Publication Data

Luitjers, Guus.
Sexbomb : the life and death of Jayne Mansfield.
Translation of: Sexbomb.
1. Mansfield, Jayne, 1933-1967. Motion picture
actors and actresses--United States--Biography.
I. Timmer, Gerard. II. Title.
PN2287.M37L8513   1988   791.43'028'0924   [B]   87-32575
ISBN 0-8065-1049-8

Published 1988 by Citadel Press
A division of Lyle Stuart Inc.
120 Enterprise Ave., Secaucus, N.J. 07094
In Canada: Musson Book Company
A division of General Publishing Co. Limited
Don Mills, Ontario

Manufactured in the United States of America

10 9 8 7 6 5 4 3 2

Introduction

I saw Jayne Mansfield only once, in the early 1960s, from a distance, in Spain. I'd rented a room in a house near Alicante, and from the terrace behind that house there was a view of the stage of an open-air nightclub that fronted the beach a few hundred meters away. Jayne's performance began at midnight, I remember. She wore a silver lamé dress, and she danced and sang. I can't remember *what* she sang, not anymore, but I do remember that you viewed her from behind, and that it was a magnificent behind, which the Americans on the terrace with me never tired of discussing.

While they talked, I found myself wondering if I'd ever actually seen any of Jayne Mansfield's films. Though she was one of the most famous personalities in the world at that time, I doubt if one in a thousand of her fans had ever seen her act. I was one of the ones who had, I recalled at last, in *The Girl Can't Help It*.

Jayne was known as the smartest dumb blonde in the world. She was a star, but you rarely came across her movies. Actually, she was more a phenomenon than a star. When she visited Holland in October 1957, she stirred up a reaction that had never been seen before, and wouldn't be matched until the Beatles came to town years later. According to one newspaper report: "After dinner, the entourage proceeded to the Asta Theater in The Hague, where more than 30 police officers were unable to hold back the enormous crowd." Escorted by American sailors in dress uniforms, Jayne was introduced to the enthusiastic spectators, and presented with a Delft-blue lamp, a doll in traditional Volendam costume, a wooden shoe containing a bottle of champagne, a ceramic plate and a silver windmill.

In 1957, Jan Cremer was seventeen years old and already well-known as a painter. A few years later he dedicated his book—*I, Jan Cremer*—to Jayne Mansfield. A few years after that they met, and began a turbulent affair. Cremer is the finest writer to have known Mansfield, and probably the only one in a position to do her memory justice in print. I hope he'll write about their relationship some day.

Meanwhile, we'll have to settle for a couple of unimpressive biographies. The volume you now hold in your hands is *not* a biography. It's a collection of Jayne's own words, words which seem to me to be those of an intelligent yet insecure woman, a woman who certainly received enormous attention, but who was never given the opportunity to make the films she was capable of making.

In my opinion, she comes across better in still photographs than in her movies. She is the personification of Everyman's ideal, the unattainable goddess, cheerful and daring, platinum blond, with that broad mouth and incredible figure. She is a phenomenon who—though gone for more than 20 years now—will always be with us.

Gerard Timmer and I would like to thank all those who participated in the creation of this book— especially Cees Aarts, Hans Auer, Jan Cremer, Peter Cuypers, Jacques Katmor, Peter and Yvonne Loeb, Thijs Ockersen, Josh Pachter, Ferry André de la Porte, Bram Reijnhout, Caroline Torenbeek and Ruth Visser.

Guus Luijters
Schagerburg/Amsterdam

Mansfield from A to Z

A

Abortion

Abortion is murder. I would never consider one, never!

Acting

To function as an actress, I have to be in love. I have to have that incentive to work.

With Leo Genn in *Too Hot to Handle*.

In *The Sheriff of Fractured Jaw.*

With Tony Randall in *Will Success Spoil Rock Hunter?*

Making up for her part in *Will Success Spoil Rock Hunter?*

With Tommy Steel in the Twickenham Studios.

Affection

A woman loves to think of herself as a little kitten to be pampered and adored. I do. I'm twenty-three, alert and eligible! I'd like to meet Bob Wagner, Bob Stack, Tyrone Power, Marlon Brando and Liberace, bless his heart. And somewhere, I hope there is a real prince for me.

In a wig.

Marlon Brando and Jack Nicholson in *The Missouri Breaks*.

With Robert Wagner.

11

Ambitions 1

I am tired of what I have been, and what I am. I am going to become a serious dramatic actress. That is my dream now. I feel that with my drive and energy and ambition, I have to accomplish more. I can't go along just being a sex symbol. I want good dramatic roles. If the studio won't give them to me, then I'll go on the stage. If I have to, I'll do my own plays with my own company.

Ambitions 2

(England, Spring 1967)
I'd like ten more babies and ten more chihuahuas and a few Academy Awards. Meanwhile, I enjoy being a sex symbol and making people happy.

◀ With Joan Collins on the Set of *The Wayward Bus*.

B

Baby

A girl can have a baby every year, and grow more beautiful with each newborn. And she can have a better figure and a lovelier skin! I am actually the living proof of my theory!

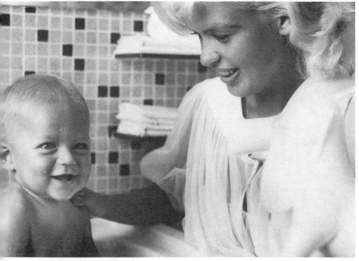

▲ Bathtime for Mickey.

▼ Baby Miklos in his crib.

▲ With daughter Mariska.

▼ Mickey Hargitay and his son.

Bath

At the height of her fame, Jayne sold her used bathwater for $10 per bottle.

Bed 1

Pictures of Jayne and Mickey sleeping on the floor of the Pink Palace were freely distributed and duly appeared in the press. The police of Laguna Beach pooled a significant sum from their combined salaries to buy Jayne Mansfield a bed.

What marvelous men—how understanding! They are really noble to buy me a bed so another man can sleep in it with me. Few men would be so generous. That proves they really love me.

Bed 2

Later, of course, came the famous heart-shaped bed.

Bedroom

Once he's happy in the bedroom, the kitchen and the living room are a cinch. Today, any intelligent girl knows that.

Blue Bruises

When Jayne appeared with black-and-blue marks, she was asked what had happened. Her answer:

Matt [Cimber] beats me. But I love it.

A meeting between Mickey Hargitay, his ex-wife and their children on the corner of 72nd Street and Fifth Avenue, New York, turns into a confrontation between Hargitay and Matt Cimber.

Books About Jayne Mansfield

Kenneth Anger
Hollywood Babylon
Phoenix, 1965
(With a censored photograph of Jayne on the cover.
Later editions use the uncensored picture and include
a new chapter on Jayne.)

George Axelrod
Will Success Spoil Rock Hunter?
New York, 1956
(The text of the Broadway play, plus an interview with
Jayne and several photos.)

Jan Cremer Krant 4 (1978)
Jan Cremer's Logboek in Beeld
(A Dutch-language magazine which includes photos
of Cremer and Mansfield and a letter from Jayne. See
also the September 1984 issue of the Dutch edition of
Playboy, in which Cremer is interviewed about—
among other things—his stormy relationship with
Jayne.)

Gerard Dauphin
Jan Cremer in New York & Jayne Mansfield
Antwerp, 1966
(Photos of Cremer, Mansfield and others in New York, dating from July 15 through September 15, 1966, plus an interview with Cremer in Dutch.)

Phil Hirsch
Hollywood Uncensored
New York, 1965
(Stories about and interviews with Tony Curtis, Tuesday Weld, Jerry Lewis, Steve McQueen, John Wayne and others. Arnold Hano's cover story on Jayne is titled, "The Sagging World of Jayne Mansfield.")

Jean-Pierre and Françoise Jackson
Jayne Mansfield
Paris, 1984
(Richly-illustrated biography and filmography. The most attractive volume on Jayne Mansfield to date. French.)

May Mann
Jayne Mansfield
New York, 1973
(An extensive but not entirely reliable—especially when discussing parapsychological phenomena—biography by a woman who knew Jayne well.)

Jayne Mansfield and Mickey Hargitay
Jayne Mansfield's Wild Wild World
Los Angeles, 1963
(An unusual volume, comprising Jayne's first attempts at autobiography filled out with chapters by Hargitay.)

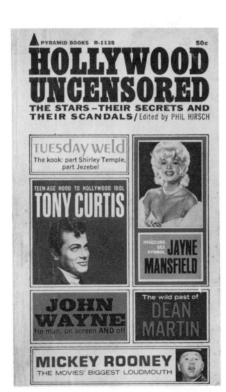

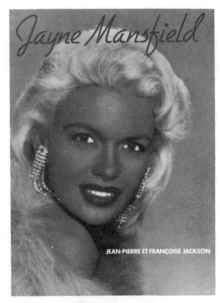

19

Danny Peary
Cult Movies
1981
(With a chapter on *The Girl Can't Help It*.)

Martha Saxton
Jayne Mansfield and the American Fifties
New York, 1975
(A catty biography.)

Raymond Strait
The Tragic Secret Life of Jayne Mansfield
Chicago, 1974
(Strait worked as Jayne's press agent for 10 years.)

Mike Wallace
Mike Wallace Asks
New York, 1958
(Short interviews with Tallulah Bankhead, Salvador Dali, Gloria Swanson, Tennessee Williams and others—including, of course, Jayne.)

Enrico Bomba 1

It was love at first sight—Rome, Bomba and I. I never want to go back to Hollywood. I feel free and loved. I was confused and lonely before I came to Rome. I never want to be lonely again. All of my life I have needed someone with experience and talent to guide my career. Bomba opens new vistas—a new career—for me.

Now I know what I need. I am sorry for Mickey, but there will be no divorce.

Enrico Bomba 2

Bomba couldn't get a divorce, he is Catholic. And I would never be a mistress. I always get married to a man I love. In that way I'm very old-fashioned.

20   With film producer Enrico Bomba. ▶

Bra

I wore brassieres until I was fourteen and then I abandoned them forever to be free. I like to feel my body free as though I am floating in air. I hate underthings. I love to sleep nude. This shocked my mother, who insisted I wear a nightgown.

Breakfast

Champagne for breakfast may sound great, but it gives you a hangover.

Breasts 1

I suddenly changed when I became twelve years old. I changed overnight from the skinny little girl to one with curves popping out all over. One of my school teachers, a man, started finding excuses to put his arms around me when he talked to me. And the boys began to whistle. My dresses became tighter, and I loved the attention. Momma kept trying to get me to wear a size larger dress or sweater or skirt to grow into. But I liked the feel of tight clothes on my body. It was like a caress.

Breasts 2

When her famous 44-18-36 turned out by British tape measures to be a 46-inch bust, why all Jayne said was:

Ooh, isn't that wonderful! I don't know how it happened but I guess it must be the five babies I've had. I'm a big girl now!

Breasts 3

A 41-inch bust and a lot of perserverance will get you more than a cup of coffee—a lot more. But most girls don't know what to do with what they've got.

Breasts 4

Frank Tashlin: "One day she came into my office wearing a tight striped sweater. 'Jayne!' I exclaimed with a slight impatience. 'Why do you wear a tight sweater like that with stripes? Don't! It looks so phony.'

"'But it's all me!' and she started to pull up her sweater."

Breasts 5

If I didn't have a large bosom, people would talk about my small one. So what's the difference? I'm glad I have a large one.

Sam Brody 1

I think I'm falling in love with him. The only trouble is he is short—a little man.

Sam Brody 2

I have no intention of ever marrying him. But he's got all of my business—everything in his briefcase. He won't give them back. He has a terrible picture he'll blackmail me with too.

C

Career 1

I realize now that I have the men on my side—but if I want to continue to be a super movie star I need women, too. I play it that way now with the P.T.A. I win both. I am going to make a pitch for the intellectuals, like presidents of the United States and kings. I will make it a point to go to every city and meet the mayor. Most of them will give me the key to the city, and lots of publicity, which is high class prestige for me. I will always take my children with me, which turns on the women.

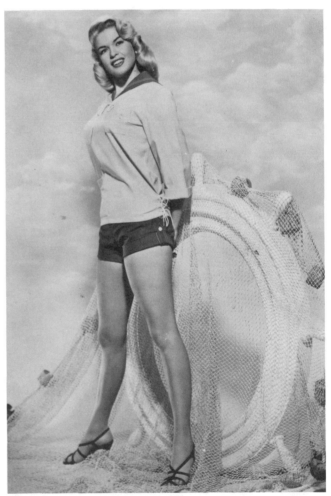

Career 2

The Studio doesn't want me to marry Mickey. Marrying him can end my contract. But I can't help it. The studio keeps telling me it will spoil everything if I marry him. Mickey's so in love with me. He's so physically exciting. I just have to marry him, career or no career.

Carnaval in Rio

(1959)
The boys just got a little excited. I really think Brazilians are wonderful, the salt of the earth. I had little red roses on the bosom of my dress. They started picking them. When the flowers were gone they went after the dress. I thought I'd be completely stripped. I was frightened for a few minutes.

On their wedding day (January 13, 1958):

24

Catholicism

After her 1962 visit to Italy, Jayne wanted to convert to Catholicism.

In Catholicism I have found everything I have dreamed a religion should be. In Rome I saw wild romances between men and women, women and women and men and men. I was surrounded with people with unreal standards. One can become confused. What's right and what is wrong? Fortunately I only observed. I never partook. I saw intelligent people living all sorts of ways. Italian men began explaining their way of life and their religion, and what it would mean to be devout and give up everything to marry me. My eyes were opened and I wanted to learn. Suddenly I knew where to turn—to God and the truth. My career will be toned down but it will continue, I believe, to become even better. I have always believed you can accomplish anything by giving just that extra effort. I will make it.

With Enrico Bomba in 1962.

25

Censorship

I think movies have to be censored. Otherwise your child's mind will be corrupted. What they hear on screen they will do in their private lives and you would have a lot of very unhappy results.

Champagne

Jayne was asked if it was true that she bathed regularly in pink champagne:

I really do. It takes many bottles—just bottles and bottles—but I do it twice a week. It gives my morale a boost.

Children

I have always said I want at least ten children. I have my five: Jayne Marie 16, Miklos 8, Zoltan 7, Maria 3, and Antonio 18 months. If God is willing, I will have five more.

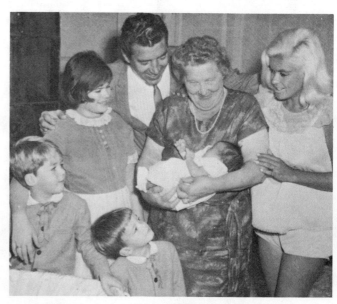

Zolton, Miklos, Jayne Marie, Mickey, Mama Hargitay, Maria and Jayne. (1964).

26

▲ Jayne's 34th birthday, with Matt Cimber and the children.

▼ Brothers and sister watch Jayne bathe Mariska.

Matt Cimber 1

Last April I reported to the Yonkers Playhouse for *Bus Stop*, and Matt was the director. He was Italian and handsome and I thought he looked like a Greek god. But he didn't really turn me on until he began to direct me, to talk to me. The fact that we fell in love is one thing. But the fact that our interests are so mutual, and he loves me so much that he will develop my career and make me a great serious actress, well...It's something like Sophia Loren and Carlo Ponti in a way. Being part of a team, instead of alone out front or before the cameras—such support is the greatest thing that has ever happened to me.

Matt Cimber 2

After exchanging wedding vows with Cimber on September 24th, 1964:

It's just too, too wonderful, almost unbelievable but it's all real. It's not a dream and I won't wake up sobbing in my pillow.

Matt Cimber 3

He's the star—such a great director. I'm the wife. I'm his lackey. He rules everything.

Matt Cimber arguing with Mickey Hargitay (see also page 17).

In London to meet the queen, Jayne bent over forwards to please the press. ▶

Jayne and Matt *en famille* (1965).

28

Clothes

The day of Jayne's presentation to the queen her dress by Charles LeMaire arrived from 20th Century-Fox by air. When she went to put the dress on, just before leaving for the Command Performance, the zipper wouldn't work. Jayne squealed:

What will I do? I ate an egg for breakfast, that's what's wrong. I can't eat anything or I gain weight.

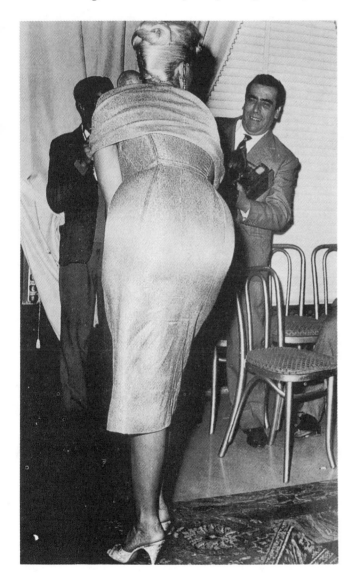

Clothes

When I went to the Girl Scout meetings in Beverly Hills, I planned. to wear a simple cloth coat. But I changed to mink finally. I didn't want to look conspicuous.

Contemporaries

Mamie van Doren, Diana Dors and Anita Ekberg

Diana Dors (1963).

▲ Mamie Van Doren (1958) with Antonio Citariollo in *La Bellissimo Gambe di Sabrina*.

◄▼ Mamie Van Doren.

Anita Ekberg.

Diana Dors. ▲▶

Anita Ekberg in *La Dolce Vita*.

With Dean Martin and Jerry Lewis in *Artists and Models*.

Anita Ekberg (1960) with Federico Fellini.

▲ Diana Dors at the premiere of *Sunset Boulevard* (1950).

Covers

NEUE
JLLUSTRIERTE

Marilyn in Gefahr?

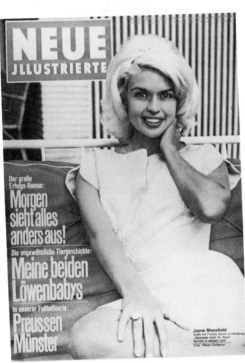

NEUE
JLLUSTRIERTE

Der große
Erfolgs-Roman:
Morgen
sieht alles
anders aus!

Die ungewöhnliche Tiergeschichte:
Meine beiden
Löwenbabys

In unserer Fußballserie:
Preussen
Münster

Jayne Mansfield
dreht mit Freddy Quinn in Hamburg
"Heimweh nach St. Pauli"
Bericht in diesem Heft.
Foto: Klaus Collignon

VROUWENJUNGLE

met
JAYNE
MANSFIELD

Collectie : DE FILMROMAN

CABARET *Quarterly*
50

EXCITING PICTURE STORIES
ON CABARET QUEENS:

LEE SHARON
JUNE HARLOW
SHARON KNIGHT

with

BEA SWEET
SANDRA POULS
IN FULL COLOR!

PINUP
ALBUM

AFTER-DARK
VISITS
TO GLAMOUR
SPOTS IN
DENVER
LAS VEGAS
HONOLULU

VOLUME SEVEN

Jan Cremer Interview

Playboy: Tell us about Jayne Mansfield.

Cremer: Simple. She was an idol of mine, a little boy's dream, even though she was only three or four years older than me. I had the idea she was a tasty little dish.

Playboy: And? Was she?

Cremer: Yeah. Everyone was nuts about Marilyn Monroe around then, but she wasn't for me. I know her type. Works in a fast-food restaurant making French fries, really sweet, beautiful girls, but you can't talk with them, they don't have anything to say. Jayne Mansfield was different. I could have fun with her, she had a sense of humor that blended perfectly with my own. We had a lot in common. We were the same sign, we actually had the same birthday.

Playboy: How did you meet her?

Cremer: I dedicated *I, Jan Cremer* to her, and my agent thought it'd be a good idea to get a picture of us together. And it's really true, the second we met in New York it was love at first sight. It was like we'd known each other forever. After they'd shot the publicity pictures, we went out to lunch. Then we went our separate ways, she had a rehearsal and I went back to my apartment. That evening her manager called me. He was desperate, I had to come down and see Jayne's show right away. So I went. I was honored, obviously.

Playboy: Obviously!

Cremer: I'm just an ordinary kid from a working-class Dutch neighborhood, and she's asking for me! She was an impulsive woman, and she'd decided she had to have me. I had to go to Hollywood with her, she said. I had managers, secretaries, everybody trying to

convince me, and that very evening I flew out to live with her in Hollywood.

Playboy: A personal question. What's it like to slip between the silken sheets with someone like Jayne Mansfield?

Cremer: I have to admit I was flattered. The first time you find yourself in bed with the world's number-one sex symbol, you catch yourself thinking: If only my friends could see me now! The kids from my neighborhood, the ones who used to laugh at me when I swore I wasn't going to settle for little Marie, the farmer's daughter, I was going to marry a famous movie star. I was proud, you know? Like I'd just won some kind of medal. It was weird. You're lying there, that voluptuous body next to you in the heart-shaped bed. And let me tell you, she was a beautiful girl, like a Scandinavian goddess. All those lousy rumors they spread, none of that was true: that body was 100 percent Jayne Mansfield. The woman I knew, the woman I slept with every night, had a beautiful body and a beautiful mind. During the day she played the Hollywood sex kitten, the typical dumb blonde. They spent hours fixing her up the way they wanted her: the cinched-in waist, the wig, the sexy treat. That was her role. But actually she was a very intelligent woman, with a couple of college degrees. Very stubborn, though. She went crazy when she didn't get her own way, she turned into a real shrew. If there wasn't a cooler filled with her favorite champagne waiting for her in her limo at seven every morning, all hell broke loose. She wouldn't set foot in the car until the champagne was there, not if they had to cross a desert to get it. It took me a while to get used to the police cars, too, the screaming sirens, the flashing lights.

Playboy: The newspapers described you as Jayne Mansfield's bodyguard and companion.

Cremer: And as her next husband. As far as being her bodyguard goes, in every South American country we visited, these strange little secret policemen in moustaches and brilliantined hair would push guns on me and put me in charge of a half-dozen or a dozen military cops. My own platoon of MP's. It was interesting, at first, roaming around South America, the rain forests, the pampas, chatting with presidents and escaped war criminals. But sooner or later you want to get back to painting and writing. She couldn't stand the thought of my going off on my own, and I couldn't stand giving up my freedom. Some men don't worry about that. Her previous husbands didn't care, it probably didn't bother them, but I wouldn't stand for it. Not from anyone, I don't care if it's the pope's daughter. I'll just jump in the ocean and start swimming. But she tried everything she could think of to keep me with her. She decided she was going to marry me. She was determined to have me for a husband, and it reached a point where I just couldn't get away from her. I could't even get hold of my passport. It was in there with the passports of all the people in her entourage, the whole publicity circus, and the guy in charge was under orders not to release my own passport to me. I wasn't allowed to leave.

One morning I flew from Caracas to Curaçao, and when I landed there, bright and early, the governor and a naval guard were there to meet me. It turned out Jayne had just been arrested back in Caracas, for jewel theft, they said. But that was crap, naturally. It didn't make sense for me to go back, they were holding her prisoner there. So I went to Amsterdam and then back to America, where I met another girl, a ballerina. I wound up marrying her. For about half a year I had all kinds of problems with Mansfield. As soon as she got back to New York she came looking for me, she couldn't stand it that I was living with another woman. There were terrible scenes, all-night phone calls when she was on tour in Vietnam. When she came back to New York again, she'd sit outside my door all night, throw rocks through my windows. I finally got away from her when I went to Europe with my dancer.

I'll never forget the day I bought an American newspaper in Nice and saw the headline: "Mansfield Dead in Car Crash." Two days before, we'd spent another couple of hours on the phone together. The first thing I said when I read about the accident—and I know this may sound cold, now—was it was actually the best solution for her, because she could never have become the person she wanted to be. That was the end of a pretty turbulent period for me.

D

Dancing

Mickey has a 52-inch chest expansion and I measure over 40 inches and we both have short arms. All this makes dancing difficult.

Death 1

Maybe when I win an Academy Award, then I can die. I don't want to die.

Death 2

(1964)
I wish it would all end, right now, right here. This minute. What a mess I've made of my life.

Death 3

About the Forest Lawn Cemetery:
This has to be the only spot in Hollywood where there aren't any troubles. This is the only place in town where I've found contentment.

Debut

(Female Jungle, 1954)
I was beside myself with joy. At last a foot in the door and as a star, too! I loved me up there on the screen. Being an actress. And a star! "I love you Jayne Mansfield" I told my "image." "I'll work hard for you! Nothing or no one, could ever make me let you down."'

Dirty Language

I dislike intensely dirty stories. Vulgar language and obscenities embarrass me. Sexy talk with a detached natural innocence, since it concerns a force in life as vital as breathing, I find amusing. Sometimes I shock my maid, Linda, when she comes in with my breakfast tray. I'll say softly: "Linda, did you ball David [her boyfried] last night?" She gets so embarrassed. Sometimes I feel the need to shock people. A little ballsy talk is as far as I ever go.

Dream

There's an old adage: "Be careful of what you wish or it will surely come true." My dream was to become a glamorous film star, and now I find it isn't worth it.

E

Eating

A London columnist wrote: "Jayne is too FAT. We love our Diana Dors, who is svelte."

Okay, so I won't eat.

On the town in London, September 18, 1959.

F

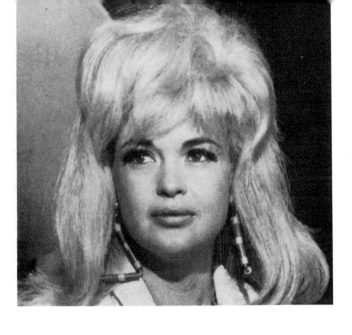

Fame 1

Before going to the bathroom at a gas station:
When I do it, that man can put up a sign over the ladies' room saying, "Jayne Mansfield peed here."

Fame 2

Back from the bathroom:
Let's bottle it and sell it.

Father

My father's death made a great impression on me. I was always asking to go to the cemetery to visit his grave. I'd sit there and talk to him. I'd cry and cry. "Daddy, you understand me and Momma doesn't," I'd sob. I'd lay on the grass of his grave and kiss the grass over him. He'd know I was kissing him. He was the only man I ever knew who really loved me unselfishly—who never used me for personal gain.

Favorite Man

He must be artistic, must have succeeded in his field, must be an exciting strong personality. It would help if he had charcoal gray hair and blue eyes, but brown eyes would be all right. I prefer men between the ages of forty-eight and fifty.

▲ Admirer Don Graham drinks champagne from Jayne's shoe.

◀ With Cary Grant.

Figure

Just think how wonderful it would be if I didn't have to be a consistent 118 pounds. Nobody would care if my waist was 19 or 29. I would do a lot of things differently—and yet, I'd still do a lot of things the same as I have. I'd still have the animals—dogs, cats, birds—and I'd still eat a lot of fresh fruit and vegetables right out of my own garden.

Films

Female Jungle

1954 (U.S.A.) 56 min.
With Lawrence Tierney, John Carradine, Burt Carlisle.
Producer: Burt Kaiser. Screenplay: Bruno Ve Sota and Burt Kaiser. Director: Bruno Ve Sota.

Actress Candy Price (Jayne Mansfield) is murdered, and a drunken policeman (Lawrence Tierney) is found at the scene. Naturally, the cop is the principal suspect, and must discover the real murderer to prove his own innocence.

This was Jayne's first film role. Frank Worth, who worked for the photo-press agency INP, helped her get the part. Jayne was hired, and earned $100 per week. The picture was originally titled *Hangover*.

"I had to portray a very sexy streetwalker, sensual and wicked. The film had to be made quickly, in less than ten days. I earned less than two hundred dollars from it. But I enjoyed every minute of it, even though I had to lie on a very hot streetcorner for one hour or had to play my own corpse. The budget didn't allow any stand-ins or dummies."

Illegal

1955 (U.S.A.) 88 min.
With Edward G. Robinson, Nina Foch, Hugh Marlow, Robert Ellenstein.
Producer: Frank Rosenberg. Screenplay: W.R. Burnett and James R. Webb, from a novel by Frank J. Collins. Director: Lewis Allen.

Remake of James Flood and Elliot Nugent's 1932 film, *The Mouthpiece*, which starred Warren William and Sidney Fox. *Illegal* was scripted by W.R. Burnett, who also wrote *Little Caesar, High Sierra* and *The Asphalt Jungle*.

A brilliant D.A. (Edward G. Robinson) realizes too late that he's sent an innocent man to the electric chair. He quits his job and starts drinking heavily, and winds up serving a prison term himself. After his release, he goes to work as a lawyer for the mob. Finally he decides that an honest death is preferable to a criminal life.

Jayne plays a nightclub singer who testifies against her boyfriend, one of the mobsters. The film was well received, but her part was so small that she wasn't mentioned in the reviews.

Pete Kelly's Blues

1955 (U.S.A.) 95 min.
With Jack Webb, Janet Leigh, Edmund O'Brian, Peggy
Lee, Ella Fitzgerald, Lee Marvin.
*Producer: Mark VII Ltd. Screenplay: Richard L.
Breen. Director: Jack Webb.*

A gangster forces jazz trumpet player and
bandleader Pete Kelly (Jack Webb) to take care of his
alcoholic girlfriend (Peggy Lee). Webb falls in love
with Janet Leigh and they defy the gangster.
Meanwhile, Peggy Lee's condition deteriorates to the
point that even her boyfriend gives up on her.

Excellent film, in which Peggy Lee sings "He Needs
Me," "Somebody Loves Me," and "Sugar," and Ella
Fitzgerald sings "Heard-Hearted Hannah" and "Pete
Kelly's Blues."

Jayne, not easy to recognize here, plays a cigarette
girl in a nightclub. She's on screen for 20 seconds.
Jack Webb asks her what she is selling, and she
answers, "Anything you want."

Hell on Frisco Bay

1955 (U.S.A.) 98 min.
With Edward G. Robinson, Alan Ladd, Paul Stuart,
Anthony Caruso.
*Producer: Jaguar Productions. Screenplay: Sydney
Boehm and Martin Rackin, from a novel by W.P.
McGivern. Director: Frank Tuttle.*

Alan Ladd plays an ex-cop who's spent five years in
Sing Sing for a murder he did not commit. On his
release, he goes after the real killer, who turns out to
be dead. Edward G. Robinson, who masterminded
the crime (and many others), is still alive, though.
Ladd gets his revenge, then begins a new life with his
wife (Joanne Dru).

Jayne's first appearance as the dumb blonde. She
visits a nightclub with Anthony Caruso. Ladd takes
Caruso to the men's room and beats him up. Jayne,
left alone at their table, is approached by a man who
offers to take her home. "Do you have any
transportation?" she asks. "No," he answers, "but I do
have a whip."

The Burglar

1955 (U.S.A.) 90 min.
With Dan Duryea, Martha Vickers, Peter Capell,
Stewart Bradley.
*Producer: Louis W. Kellerman. Screenplay: David
Goodis from his novel* The Burglar. *Director: Paul
Wendkos.*

With the help of Jayne Mansfield, Dan Duryea
commits a well-planned burglary that winds up
netting them nothing but a single necklace. Stewart
Bradley, representing the police, is sent after the
necklace, but he's just as crooked as Duryea. He tries
to seduce Mansfield, who grew up with Duryea and
loves him, and sends his own girlfriend (Martha
Vickers) after the burglar, figuring that one or the
other of them will find out where the necklace has
been hidden. Bradley eventually murders Duryea and
gets the necklace, but is caught by his honest
colleagues.

Warner Brothers loaned Jayne out for this
independent production, in which she played her first
major (and effective) role.

"*The Burglar* differs completely from everything else
that I have done so far. It is a very serious part--no
make-up. It has nothing to do with my body; my breasts
aren't involved. It presents me as an actress. If they
paid more attention to my breasts, that would conflict
with the attention I need as an actress. I play a tragic
part, not a comic part."

The Girl Can't Help It

1956 (U.S.A.) 97 min.
With Tom Ewell, Edmund O'Brien, Henry Jones, and Julie London, Fats Domino, Gene Vincent, Eddie Cochran, The Platters & Little Richard.
Producer: Frank Tashlin. Screenplay: Frank Tashlin and Herbert Baker from a story by Garson Kanin. Director: Frank Tashlin.

After her starring role opposite Dan Duryea in *The Burglar*, there was no doubt about it: Jayne was on her way up. but Warner Bros. inexplicably let her go.

"I thought I owned the whole world. I was sure that if I returned to Warner Bros. they would offer me only leading parts in important movies. On the set everybody was reading the trade papers that they would send us from Hollywood, and someone said, 'Hey, Jayne, here's a big story about you.' With a smile on my face I took the newspaper and read: 'Warner Bros. drops Jayne Mansfield.' "

She couldn't believe it. She called her agent, who confirmed the story. He told her not to worry, that he could get better parts for her on Broadway.

"I do not want to play on Broadway," I said. "I Want to be a star in Hollywood."

In spite of her wariness of Broadway, Jayne went to New York and auditioned for George Axelrod's play, *Will Success Spoil Rock Hunter?* She got the part, and the show opened on October 12, 1955. As the curtain rises, Jayne is lying on a massage table with a towel wrapped around her. The moment audiences saw her, they were hers. The play became the hit of the year, and Jayne was its main attraction. Her name was in the newspapers daily, she appeared on television talk shows, her picture could be seen in every store in New York. *Will Success Spoil Rock Hunter?* lasted for 452 performances, and its run was only broken when 20th Century-Fox—having, meanwhile, signed Jayne to a contract—picked up the film rights as a vehicle for her.

There were script problems, though, since the play was strongly critical of Hollywood, and while those problems were being worked out Jayne was featured in another film, *The Girl Can't Help It.*

Talent scout and promoter Tom Ewell has big problems. His main client (Julie London) has left him, and he winds up a drunk. But he meets a gangster (Edmund O'Brien) who assigns him to turn his girlfriend (Jayne Mansfield) into a star. Jayne has a voice like an air-raid siren, but her figure makes up for it. Her first record is a hit, but there's still trouble:

She's fallen in love with Ewell. There is, of course, a happy ending: O'Brien becomes a rock-and-roll star, and Jayne quits performing to marry Ewell.

Every scene of *The Girl Can't Help It* wears the stamp of director Frank Tashlin, who bombards his audiences with sight gags straight out of the funny pages. As Jayne walks down the street in the opening scene, the caps pop off milk bottles, and windows and eyeglasses shatter.

The Girl Can't Help It is a memorable film, a precursor of the Pop Art movement and, at the same time, a wonderful documentary on the rock-and-roll of the times: Little Richard signs the title song and "She's Got It," Fats Domino does "Blue Monday," Eddie Cochran (shortly before his tragic death) performs "Twenty Flight Rock," the Platters do "You'll Never Know," Gene Vincent contributes "Be Bop a Lula" and Julie London gets historical with "Cry Me a River."

Frank Tashlin: "I knew that Jayne was perfect for the film. I had only seen pictures of her, but I was convinced. When I met her it was love at first sight. She really cooperated. She was fantastic. The press loved her and we had interviews going on all the time. And our film was a smash hit."

And Jayne: "That 'It' in the title of course has to do with sex-appeal--what else would it mean? I play a girl that has the most gorgeous body in the whole world, but who is totally unaware of her sex-appeal. The only thing she wants to be is a wife and a mother. But sex interferes all the time. You could say that this character is really like me. That is why this is such a perfect part for me--I really understand this character."

Will Success Spoil Rock Hunter?

1957 (U.S.A.) 95 min.
With Tony Randall, Betsy Drake, Joan Blondell,
Henry Jones.
Producer: Frank Tashlin. Screenplay: Frank Tashlin.
Director: Frank Tashlin.

Rockwell Hunter (Tony Randall) makes television commercials for an ad agency. The agency is in danger of losing an important account, unless Randall can quickly develop a campaign for Stay Put lipstick. Meanwhile, in Hollywood, TV star Rita Marlowe (Jayne Mansfield) fights with her lover, Bobo Branniganski (Mickey Hargitay), and leaves for New York, where she meets up with Randall. He asks her to appear in his lipstick campaign and she agrees—but only if he'll help her make Hargitay jealous. The Stay Put campaign is a success, and the "romance" between Jayne and Randall becomes international news. In the middle of all this, Jayne runs into George Schmidlapp (Groucho Marx), the man she's *really* loved all along, the man she's been trying to forget by throwing herself into affairs with others. Jayne winds up with Schmidlapp, Randall leaves the ad biz to start a chicken farm, and everyone lives happily ever after. Especially Schmidlapp.

Jayne's performance is a perfect parody of her own real-life persona. Rita Marlowe *is* Jayne Mansfield, and it's interesting to note that in later years, Mansfield often introduced herself as Jayne Marlowe.

The film still holds up well today.

The Wayward Bus

1957 (U.S.A.) 89 min.

With Joan Collins, Dan Dailey, Rick Jason, Betty Lou Keim

Producer: Charles Bracket. Screenplay: Ivan Moffat after the novel by John Steinbeck. Director: Victor Vicas.

Twice a week, busdriver Rick Jason has the run from Rebel to San Juan; his wife (Joan Collins) stays home to operate their gas station and café. When bad weather brings one run to an unexpected halt midway, the stranded bus is filled with the classic cross-section of humanity. One of the passengers is Jayne Mansfield, who claims to be a dental assistant. It turns out she's also a model, who poses under the name Naked Truth.

After an assortment of revelations, a helicopter rescues the cast and Jayne marries fellow passenger Dan Dailey.

Frank Tashlin: "I advised her not to do the film. In God's name, what can you do when you have to sit in a bus for more than one hour?"

But *The Wayward Bus* is not a complete failure, and at least Jayne appears at her most beautiful.

ss *Them For Me*

7 (U.S.A.) 103 min.

th Cary Grant, Leif Ericson, Suzy Parker, Ray
lston.

ducer: *Jerry Wald. Screenplay: Julius Epstein after*
play by Luther Davis and the novel by Frederic
keman. Director: Stanley Donen.

uring World War II, Cary Grant and two other
cers are on leave in San Francisco. The hotels are
, and they wind up in a very expensive suite
ich had been reserved for someone else. They
ow a big party and meet various new people,
luding Jayne. But Grant falls for the icy Suzy
ker—who arrives looking for the suite's intended
st. During the course of the film, though, she
ntually succumbs to Grant's charm.

The picture features several major stars and, in Stanley Donen, a talented director, but it never quite gets off the ground.

Frank Tashlin: "Our previous two films had made a lot of money and Jane was ready for her next pricture. 'A film with Cary Grant,' she said, very excited. 'Can you imagine, me in a film with Cary Grant." She was so happy. I begged her: Don't do it, Jayne. Don't play second fiddle to Suzy Parker (who was also in this movie). I pointed out that Suzy ends up with Grant, but Jayne did the movie anyhow."

Jayne was very pleased with Grant: "He is one of the most fantastic men I have ever met. Every day he sends me little gifts to cheer me up."

Grant's praise for her, however, was less than enthusiastic. "A potential Mae West," he said of her. Grant had had his experiences with Mae West.

The Sheriff of Fractured Jaw
1958 (G.B.) 103 min.
With Kenneth More, He ry Hull, William Campbell, Bruce Cabot.
Producer: Daniel M. Angel. Screenplay: Arthur Dales from a story by Jacob Ha . Director: Raoul Walsh.

Gun salesman Kenneth More leaves 19th-century London for America's Wild West. When a stage wagon is attacked by Indians, More saves the life of the chief. At the end of the journey lies the town of Fractured

Jaw, where More finds himself involved *in* a war between two ranchers and *with* the owner of the local saloon (Jayne Mansfield). With the chief's help, he brings peace to Fractured Jaw. The townspeople name him their sheriff, and—with the chief as witness—he marries Jayne.

"It was fantastic. Cowboys and Indians and all that. It is an English western, shot in Spain. I play a very different kind of girl. This completely different from the things I have done so far. She governs the little city from her saloon!"

Too Hot To Handle

1959 (G.B.) 100 min.
With Leo Genn, Karlheinz Boehm, Christopher Lee, Kai Fisher.
Producer: Phil C. Samuel. Screenplay: Herbert Kretzner from an idea by Harry Lee. Director: Terence Young.

Midnight Franklin (Jayne Mansfield) is the star attraction at The Pink Flamingo, a nightclub in the Soho section of London owned by Leo Genn. Though Leo and Jayne are in love, he refuses to tell her about his past. Into this situation comes a French journalist (Karlheinz Böhm), who succeeds in discovering the skeleton in Genn's closet. Genn's main competitor sees his chance and ruins The Pink Flamingo, and Genn himself goes on the counter-offensive. As a result, he and Jayne wind up separated.

The film's main attractions are the song-and-dance

numbers performed in the nightclub. Jayne, shoehorned into incredible costumes, sings "Too Hot to Handle," "You Were Made For Me" and "Monsoon and Midnight." It's all terribly kitschy, and recommended for devoted fans only.

Interestingly, author Ian Fleming plays a minor role. Several years later, director Terrence Young helmed Fleming's first James Bond movie, *Dr. No.*

Too Hot to Handle was banned in America; the censors insisted that Jayne's costumes were too revealing. She suggested hand-painting more clothing onto the offending celluloid, but budget restrictions made that solution impossible.

The Challenge

1959 (G.B.) 92 min.
With Anthony Quayle, Carl Mohner, Peter Reynolds,
John Bennet.
Producer: John Temple-Smith. Screenplay: John
Gilling. Director: John Gilling.

Jayne is the leader of a gang of burglars. Anthony
Quayle, a member of the gang, falls in love with her.
After a job, Quayle hides the loot but is turned in by
Carl Mohner and goes to prison. Mohner takes over
the gang, and spends five years searching for the
missing money. On Quayle's release, Mohner kidnaps
his six-year-old son in an attempt to force Quayle to
reveal the location of the loot. Working with Jayne and
Scotland Yard, though, Quayle gets back his son and
breaks up the gang.

Although the picture is mediocre, Jayne has some
impressive scenes, like the one where a member of the
gang discovers that she is a woman.

Another nice moment comes when the infuriated
Mohner starts ripping off Jayne's clothing, revealing
her lovely breasts. She has a chance to sing, too, this
time a number called "The Challenge of Love."

"They needed three hours to convince me to do the
bedroom scene without a bra."

Gli Amori Di Ercole

1960 (It./Fr.) 94 min.
With Mickey Hargitay, Moire Orfei, Massimo Serato,
Rene Dary.
*Producer: Grandi Schermi Italiani. Screenplay: Doria
Allessandro Continenza. Director: Carlo Ludovico
Bragaglia.*

Hercules' wife is murdered. On his way to avenge
her death, he meets Jayne and falls in love with her.
His royal rival accuses him of killing Jayne's fiancé, so
Hercules sets out after the real murderer. During his
search, his life is threatened by the Hydra of Lerne.
Hippolyte, the Queen of the Amazons, saves him. In
order to seduce him she takes on Jayne's appearance.
Hercules discovers that Hippolyte changes her lovers
into trees when she's had enough of them, so he flees.
He goes back to Jayne, but she's been kidnapped. He
tracks her down and, after a terrible battle with a
cyclops, they live happily ever after.

This picture demonstrates clearly that Mickey
Hargitay wasn't much of an actor, and that Jayne had
her off-days, too.

It Happened In Athens

1960 (U.S.A.) 100 min.
With Trax Colton, Nico Minardos, Bob Mathias,
Maria Xenia.
Producer: James S. Elliot. Screenplay: Laslo Vadnay.
Director: Andrew Marton.

It's 1896, and the Olympic Games are about to begin
in the Greek capital. Spiridon Loues heads for Athens
to compete in the marathon. On the way, he
encounters Christina Gratsos, Jayne's personal
servant. Jayne, a famous Athenian actress and in love
with Lieutenant Vinardos, announces that she will
marry the man who takes the gold medal in the
marathon. Naturally, she expects her lieutenant to
win—and, obviously, it's Spiridon who winds up
victorious. But there's a happy ending after all:
Spiridon marries Christina and Jayne winds up with
the lieutenant.

"The actress I play has platinum-blond hair, because
she has been to Paris and saw the latest fashion over
there. Or, well, she imitates Jean Harlow and Mae
West--or were those two around yet in those days?"

The George Raft Story

1961 (U.S.A.) 105 min.
With Ray Danton, Julie London, Barrie Chase, Frank Gorshin.
Producer: Ben Schwalb for Allied Artists. Screenplay: Crane Wilbur. Director: Joseph M. Newman.

Dancer George Raft (played by Ray Danton) finds himself involved with the criminal underworld. After a conflict with gangster boss Frank Donatella (Joe de Santis), he is exiled to Hollywood, where he wins a role in the film *Scarface* and becomes famous. He lives with actress Lisa Lang (Jayne Mansfield) in a huge villa, but when his mother dies he deserts her. His career slides downhill until he is offered a part in *Some Like It Hot* and becomes famous again.

A strange blend of fact and fiction, with excellent performances by Neville Brand as Al Capone (a role he played earlier in *The Scarface Mob*) and by Brad Dexter as Bugsy Siegel. The Lisa Lang character played by Jayne is based on Betty Grable, George Raft's longtime girlfriend.

Panic Button

1962 (U.S.A.) 90 min.
With Maurice Chevalier, Eleanor Parker, Michael Connors, Akim Tamiroff.
Producer: Ron Gorton. Screenplay: Hal Biller from an original story by Ron Gorton. Director: George Sherman.

A businessman plans to solve his tax problems by financing a film version of *Romeo and Juliet*. He hires Maurice Chevalier and Jayne Mansfield to play the title roles, and Akim Tamiroff to direct. The finished film is shown at the Venice Festival, where it's considered a witty parody and awarded a Golden Lion.

Promises, Promises!

1963 (U.S.A.) 75 min.
With Tommy Noonan, Marie McDonald, Mickey Hargitay, Fritz Feld.
Producer: Tommy Noonan, Donald F. Taylor. Screenplay: William Welch after a play by Edna Sheklow. Director: King Donovan.

A TV-scriptwriter (Tommy Noonan) and his wife (Jayne Mansfield) are on an around-the-world cruise. The next cabin is occupied by a couple (Mickey Hargitay and Marie McDonald) who are hoping that rest and relaxation will restore hubby's potency so that wifey can get pregnant. Needless to say, complications arise. Ultimately, *both* women wind up pregnant, and the eternally-drunk Noonan can't decide which man is the father of which child.

Promises, Promises! achieved notoriety because of Jayne's two nude scenes; in 1963 it was unusual for a star of her magnitude to agree to appear in the buff. A photo layout in *Playboy* added to the picture's fame—although it should be mentioned that most of the film's viewers saw *only* the nude scenes, on 8mm filmclips, in the privacy of their own living rooms.

"If you know me a little, you will agree that it is a rather prudish sort of movie."

Jayne sings "Lu-Lu-Lu" and "Promise Her Anything."

Spree

1963 (U.S.A.) 84 min.
With Vic Damone, Juliet Prowse, Mickey Hargitay, Constance Moore.
Producer: Caroll Case and Hal Roach, Jr. Screenplay: Sydney Field. Directors: Mitchell Leisen and Walon Green.

Pseudo-documentary about Las Vegas, with most of the filming done in the Tropicana and the Dunes.

Jayne does a strip-tease and sings "Promise Her Anything."

Heimweh Nach St. Pauli

1963 (East Germany) 104 min.
With Freddy Quinn, Ulrich Haupt, Bill Ramsey, Enna Setmer.
Producer: Rapid-Constantin. Screenplay: Gustav Kampendonk. Director: Werner Jacobs.

An East German production which, according to May Mann, is not at all bad. It never had a general American release, though, and was shown only in Yorktown, a German neighborhood in New York.

Jayne sings two German songs, one of them a duet with Nelson Sardelli, her lover at the time the picture was filmed.

Dog Eat Dog

1963 (U.S.A.-It.-D.D.R.) 84 min.
With Cameron Mitchell, Elizabeth Flickenschildt,
Isa Mirando, Dody Heath.
Producer: Carl Szokol. Screenplay: Robert Hill and
Michael Elkins from When Strangers Meet *by Robert*
Bloomfield. Directors: Ray Nazzaro and Albert
Sugsmith.

Two gangsters rob a bank of a million dollars and
flee to an island in the Adriatic Sea, accompanied by a
sexy starlet (Jayne Mansfield). Each member of the trio
plots to get away with *all* the money, which leads to
violence and, ultimately, death.

Jayne's role is similar to the one she played in *The*
Challenge. This is a more suspenseful film, though,
largely because Cameron Mitchell makes a better
co-star than did Anthony Quayle. A competent thriller.

Primitive Love

1964 (It.) 83 min.
With Franco Franchi, Ciccio Inbrassia, Luigi Scattini,
Mickey Hargitay.
Producer: Dick Randall, Joel Holt and Fulvio Lusicano.
Screenplay: Luigi Scattini and Amedeo Sollazzo from
a story by Luigi Scattini. Director: Luigi Scattini.

Jayne plays an anthropologist who's made a film in
an attempt to demonstrate that the language of love is
universal, that primitive and civilized people make
love in the same way. She shows her film to a
professor, who remains unconvinced of the validity of
her thesis—until Jayne herself performs a striptease
for him, which impresses him much more than did
her movie.

Lots of stock footage of marital practices from
around the world, plus scenes of mating animals.
Jayne interacts with an Italian comedy duo popular at
the time, but none of it really goes anywhere.

Much of the material was later recycled in *The Wild*
Wild World of Jayne Mansfield.

The Loved One

1964 (U.S.A.) 116 min.
With Jonathan Winters, Robert Morse, Milton Berle,
John Gielgud, Rod Steiger.
*Producer: Martin Ramsonoff. Screenplay: Terry
Southern and Christopher Isherwood after the novel
by Evelyn Waugh. Director: Tony Richardson.*

A fine satire on the funeral business, in which a
young British poet goes to work at a Hollywood
cemetery.

All of Jayne's scenes, unfortunately, wound up on
the cutting-room floor.

The Fat Spy

1965 (U.S.A) 75 min.
With Phyllis Diller, Jack E. Leonard, Brian Donlevy,
Jordan Christopher.
*Producer: Everett Rosenthal. Screenplay: Matthew
Andrews. Director: Joseph Cates.*

On a small island off the coast of Florida,
representatives of a cosmetics manufacturer are
searching for the Fountain of Youth; their boss's
daughter (Jayne Mansfield) has come along for the
ride. They find the Fountain, but no one's allowed to
drink from it.

Supposedly a hysterical film, which leaves no stone
unturned in its quest for laughs. Camp?

Las Vegas Hillbillies

1965 (U.S.A.) 90 min.
With Ferlin Husky, Mamie van Doren, Don Bowman,
Billie Bird.
*Producer: Larry E. Jackson. Screenplay: Larry E.
Jackson. Director: Arthur C. Pierce.*

Ferlin Husky inherits a Las Vegas casino, and on
his way there he meets up with Jayne. Once arrived,
they discover that the "casino" is actually nothing but
an old barn. Together with Mamie Van Doren, they
organize a Country-and-Western show, which is a big
success. Ferlin marries Mamie, and Jayne becomes the
manager of the casino.

Jayne hated Mamie Van Doren, and they never once
spoke to each other during the making of the film.

Single Room Furnished

1966 (U.S.A.) 93 min.

With Dorothy Keller, Fabian Dean, Billy M. Green, Terri Messina.

Producer: Michael Musto. Screenplay: Michael Musto after a play by Gerald Sanford. Director Matteo Ottaviano (Matt Cimber).

Three stories in one: Johnie (Jayne Mansfield) is married, but her husband deserts her when she becomes pregnant. She changes her name to Mae and takes a job as a waitress. She falls in love, but her fiancé leaves her just as they're about to get married. So Mae changes her name to Eileen and becomes a prostitute.

This film wasn't released until after Jayne's death. By the time it appeared, a 15-minute introduction by Mansfield admirer Walter Winchell had been tacked on.

A Guide For The Married Man

1966 (U.S.A.) 89 min.

With Walter Matthau, Robert Morse, Inger Stevens, Claire Kelly.

Producer: Frank McCarthy. Screenplay: Frank Tarloff from his book. Director: Gene Kelly.

After 14 years of marriage, Walter Matthau is ready for a change. He takes infidelity lessons from a friend (Robert Morse), and the result is a large number of comic scenes. By film's end, of course, Matthau decides to go back to his wife.

A high-spirited film, largely due to Matthau's fine performance and Gene Kelly's inspired direction. Jayne appears in one brief scene with Terry-Thomas; though short, it's an effective bit.

The Wild Wild World of Jayne Mansfield
1966 (U.S.A.)
Producer: Dick Randall for Southeastern Pictures.
Screenplay: Charles Ross. Director: Arthur Knight.

A pseudo-biography including scenes from *Primitive Love* and *Promises, Promises!*, plus footage of Jayne in Paris and Rome and at the Cannes Film Festival. She shows Mickey Hargitay through the Pink Palace and judges a Jayne Mansfield lookalike contest for transvestites. Jayne herself provides the voiceover narration.

Fotomodelling

I went to the modeling agencies—all of them. Some gave me jobs. But not enough. I was the sexy type, and I could pose in bikinis. But I soon learned that movie starlets would pose in them free, to get their pictures in the papers. And when you did get a job, you had to fight for your honor. Whoever hired you always had sex on his mind. I was a married woman, although I never said so. I had no intention of becoming an adultress. My religious training from home was still strongly with me.

Jayne wore furs even in the middle of the summer. ▶

G

Clark Gable

I want lots of babies. I'm good and I'm healthy. I want to become a princess—or even a queen—if there is a king for me. There's Clark Gable.

God

I guess a lot of people think that a girl who shows her bosom and wears tight dresses can't be close to God. God has always been close to me. Only he knew what was in my heart.

H

Mickey Hargitay 1

I knew I wanted Mickey ten minutes after we were introduced at the Latin Quarter. We have been so close ever since. I've had to go it alone, with my family and Paul putting obstacles in my path all the way. Mickey wants to devote himself to helping my career. It's like I've been pulling a huge wagon alone. Now there will be two of us.

Mickey Hargitay 2

Mickey's so in love with me. He's so physically exciting. I am so turned on by him. I wouldn't trade him for any of the millionaires or the titled men I met in London or anywhere.

Mickey Hargitay 3

At their wedding on January 13, 1958:
   Ours is a real marriage, born of real love and·union. It takes place within, and there our heaven is.

Mickey Hargitay 4

By the beginning of 1960, the marriage was in trouble:

Mickey is turning into just a husband. He gets up early and wants to go to bed early. I have to go out and see and be seen or I'm dead. I don't want just a dull unexciting man in my life. I want, and have to have, a lover!

Jean Harlow

Jayne wanted to play the lead in the screen biography of Jean Harlow:

I have thousands of letters here, from people all over the world, saying I am the perfect Harlow... even naturally have her mannerisms of caressing my body and my arms in that way. But no, they can't see me playing the dramatic side of Harlow's life.

Jean Harlow.

▲ In *Primitive Love*

Hollywood 1

About her first visit, as a child, to Hollywood:

It was the greatest thing that ever happened to me. I stood on the corner of Hollywood and Vine one afternoon, and I knew someday this town would belong to me.

Hollywood 2

Some little girls get lost in Hollywood, but they would have been lost in their hometowns, or anywhere else.

Hollywood 3

Hollywood is the same as any other place when it comes to love, marriage, and divorce...some people have trouble staying married and some people have trouble staying single.

Hollywood 4

Even while Paul was unpacking the car, I went to a telephone booth and began putting dimes in, making calls to agents listed in the Hollywood directory. I didn't have any luck until I decided to call Paramount Studios direct. I was put through to Mr. Milt Lewis, the talent chief. I told his secretary I was a beauty contest winner from Dallas, and had newly arrived to become a movie star. She was so surprised, she gave me an appointment. I worked hard to impress them. I looked like a sexpot but I could read Shakespeare. I prepared some lines from *Romeo and Juliet* and Shaw's *Saint Joan*. Everyone was impressed and surprised! I thought I had a contract when they gave me a screen test. But I was never called back. Every time I called I was told: "Don't call us, we'll call you when we have something."

Husbands 1

On Mickey and Cimber:
I would have been better off if I had rented them instead of marrying them. It would have been a lot cheaper.

With Matt Cimber (middle).

With Mickey Hargitay.

With Matt Cimber (left).

With Hargitay (left) and Cimber (right).

Husbands 2

See Paul Mansfield, Mickey Hargitay and Matt Cimber.

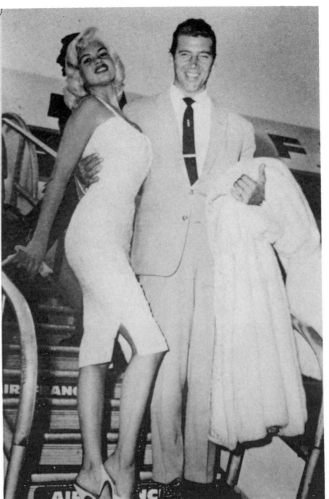

With Paul Mansfield.

▲ With Hagarty and ▼ Cimber.

I

I 1

I have always considered my career self and my personal self as two different and separate people. There's Jayne Mansfield at home, a wife and devoted mother, and there's Jayne the sex symbol, which is my career. I have always kept them completely apart and separate.

I 2

No one wants to see or read about a dull subject. I don't consider myself a dull subject.

I 3

I looked at the little kid in the mirror with the mousey brown hair, horn-rimmed glasses, and I vowed that I would be beautiful some day. And I would be a movie star. A Big Star!

I.Q. 1

I had few playmates. The ones I had seemed childish. I was restless and I grew bored easily. At the University of Texas it was discovered I had an I.Q. of 163. Everyone laughed when I'd mention it. I cooled it. In Hollywood, I realized it would ruin my feminine, sexy "image." Who wants a brainy blonde?

I.Q. 2

A girl has to have brains to get somewhere in this world. Brains are a handicap for a woman if obvious. I only use mine secretly.

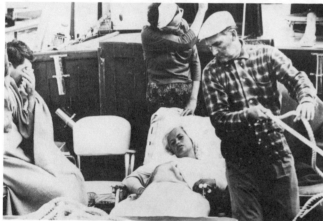

In February 1962, Jayne was stranded on an uninhabited coral reef for 20 hours with husband Mickey Hargitay and a friend when their boat capsized. They were rescued by a group of fishermen, who brought them to Rose Island.

L

Life

There are few rules and moral conventions. It is adventure, adventure every minute of the day and night.

Lingerie

Fashion designer Oleg Cassini disapproved of Jayne's insistence on wearing pink, suggesting she dress in black instead.

Good. Then I'll be able to wear black dresses over my black lingerie.

At the Tropicana (Las Vegas), May 16, 1959.

Sophia Loren 1

I was invited to a party in honor of Sophia Loren, which was given at Romanoff's. I selected a very low-cut dress--it was the only one that wasn't at the cleaner's or being repaired. Okay, I did not wear a bra--I never wear a bra--and besides that, there are more women who do not wear a bra under an evening dress than there are that do. When I arrived at Romanoff's, I immediately went over to Sophia Loren's table to say hello. She was sitting and I was standing, so I bowed a little to say something to her and immediately the photographers showed up. I had no idea of how much of myself was showing. It occurred to me only when I saw Sophia's face, when she was looking at my dress. It was too late to change anything, so I let the photographers do their job and then I returned to my own table. I have enemies who say that I did all this on purpose to steal the show from Sophia Loren, but that is not true. But I did show Shophia Loren that American women also have breasts.

Sophia Loren 2

After the incident with the photograph Loren said she would never wear a dress like that.

Maybe she can't afford to wear dresses like this. You know if you wave a flag it has to have something to hold it up. It doesn't just stay up by itself.

Love

Shortly before her death:

Esquire asked me if I had a new love. I replied, "Would you expect me to stay home every night with a book?"

M

Paul Mansfield

Jayne and Paul were married on January 28, 1950.

Paul J. Mansfield was one of the best-looking students in school. I saw him at church. I made it a point to walk out when he did. He had to notice me. I smiled and we became acquainted. Two months later we were married. Since I was fourteen we had to lie about my age for the license. But I looked easily eighteen.

Paul Mansfield (left).

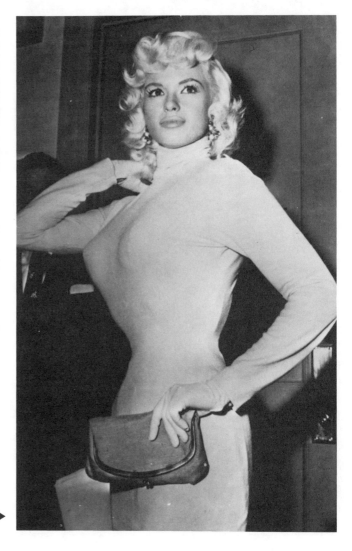

Leaving the courthouse where she divorced Mansfield (October 26, ▶ 1956).

Men 1

I have never met a man who didn't make a pass at me.

▲ With Mickey Hargitay in Berlin (1961).

▼ With Cary Grant.

Jayne Mansfield en Cary Grant

Men 2

I've had a wonderful thirteen years in Hollywood. I've been able to get everything I've always wanted, except real, lasting unselfish love from a man. The Chinese, you know, wish you seven happinesses, but they only name six of them: gentle birth, pleasant childhood, good marriage, many children, prosperous business and quick death. The seventh, they tell you, is up to you. You've got to figure it out and find it for yourself.

With Kenneth Moore. ▶

▲ With David Niven.

▼ During the second international film festival in Beirut (1962).

Men 3

There's only one thing wrong with Mickey. He has no hair on his chest. Not a single hair. I'm a girl who always likes hairy men.

With Mickey and the children.

With Mickey Hargitay.

Men 4

About Mickey:

Career-wise, I know I shouldn't marry. But he has the biggest—and I'm not going to let go of it.

Jayne and Mickey.

Men 5

In 1958, Jayne came out with a list of her ten favorite bachelors. Included were:

Nick Ray the movie director, is forty-one, tall and attractive. He directed *Rebel Without a Cause*. He has that rare combination of brawn, brains and achievement. I like that.

Adlai Stevenson is a strong, powerful man and so sure of himself. I admire such strength of character. I don't know him but I'd like to.

Johnny Ray has a voice that goes right through me. I can't even think what he looks like or does, or what makes him so appealing. I just know I want to listen to him and get caught up in that old, little, white cloud.

Men 6

When a girl dates a dozen different men, she can expect ten dozen different situations. And a lot of mixups. And men who expect a girl to go to bed after a first date.

Money

People just don't pay attention to anything that's free. I should have charged them. I mean it. The more you charge, the more value they put on you.

Marilyn Monroe 1

Marilyn and I are entirely different. We've really never been in competition. I admire Marilyn and she's told me she admires me.

Marilyn Monroe 2

On being compared, once again, with Marilyn Monroe:
I don't wiggle. I walk. I am a good actress—an original. I don't know why you people like to compare me to Marilyn or that girl, what's her name, Kim Novak. Cleavage, of course, helped me a lot to get where I am. I don't know how they got there.

Marilyn
Monroe

'The photographer
said: I can tell
you this,
Marilyn Monroe
has more
sexual vibrations
than any woman that
I ever shot.'

FEBRUARY

S	M	T	W	T	F	S
					1	2
3	4	5	6	7	8	9
10	11	12	13	14	15	16
17	18	19	20	21	22	23
24	25	26	27	28		

APRIL

S	M	T	W	T	F	S
	1	2	3	4	5	6
7	8	9	10	11	12	13
14	15	16	17	18	19	20
21	22	23	24	25	26	27
28	29	30				

MARCH

S	M	T	W	T	F	S
					1	2
3	4	5	6	7	8	9
10	11	12	13	14	15	16
17	18	19	20	21	22	23
24 31	25	26	27	28	29	30

Mother 1

We had an average small white frame house in an average middle-class neighborhood in Phillipsburg, New Jersey. My mother was very strict, too strict! She had taught elementary school, and rules and regulations were natural to her. I know she loved me, but she expected perfection from a little child. I admit I was a handful right from the beginning. I had such an imagination and was always telling fabulous stories. I looked out at the hot dusty roads in the summer. I imagined they were beautiful winding roads in some far away place like the French Riviera, or in Italy. There was always a tall, dark, handsome knight coming to rescue me on his white horse. Later he came in a big white Cadillac!

Mother 2

My mother, was a lousy parent, but I always thought of her as a glamorous lady who loved to play bridge and get drunk. She hasn't changed too much. Now she's a lousy grandparent. She still drinks and plays bridge.

N

Nightclub Act

What I sell is not pure sex, but laughs, a satire on it. I always ask the wives present if I can play with their husbands for a minute, and I only kiss a few bald heads. Everyone seems to enjoy it, as they are all part of it. But one night a gentleman too deep in his cups threw me over a table and tried to rape me. They pulled him off. I was most upset. Usually they don't get that carried away.

Nude Poses

I posed nude and I have often wondered why those photos haven't come back to haunt me—or to help, as the case might be.

Nude Scenes

The censors wanted the nude scenes removed
from Promises, Promises:

    The only objections I've heard are that the scenes are
not long enough!

When PLAYBOY arrived on the set of Jayne's latest celluloid tour de force to photograph the magnificent Mansfield superstructure for its June 1963 issue, and to take the previously unreleased shots which appear in this first BEST FROM PLAYBOY, Jayne confided to us: "I posed for these scenes for one reason only. They were necessary to the development of the story line . . . It was art for art's sake—my theme for the future."

We liked the theme then; we like it still. It would be difficult to argue the fact that Jayne's willingness to repeatedly reveal her abundant charms in front of our cameras, in spite of her success as a star of stage and screen, surely paved the way for other beauties of the entertainment world—Susan Strassberg, Kim Novak, Mamie Van Doren —to reconsider their own bans against nudity and consent to lend their feminine warmth to PLAYBOY's pages.

Jayne is unashamedly proud of the gifts that Nature has generously bestowed on her, and PLAYBOY has thoroughly enjoyed its role as the exclusive chronicler of her career. Our readers can look forward to future chapters in the saga of the West Texas schoolgirl who made it big, and who will never relent in her efforts to remain the complete Jayne Mansfield.

Opposite: Jayne's final pose for the still cameras—in case they missed something.

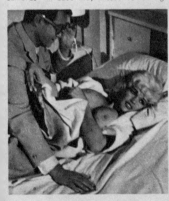

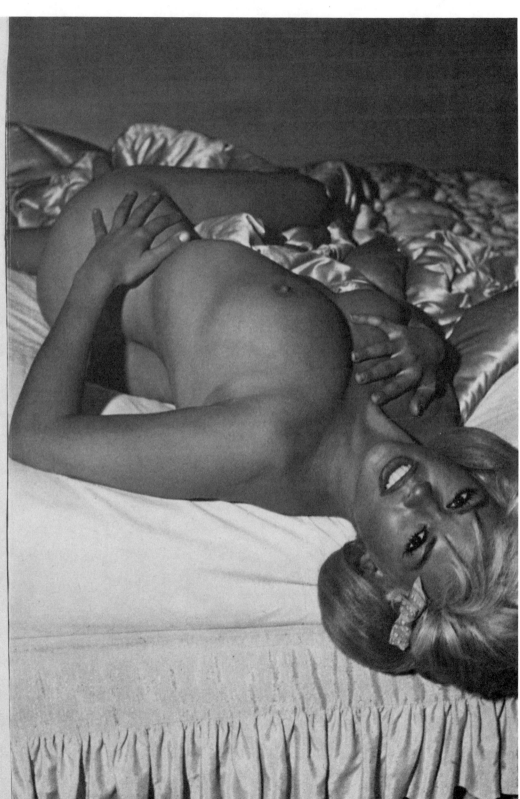

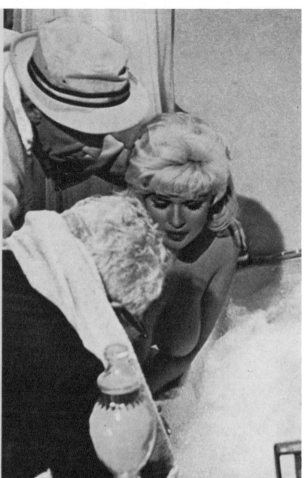

Above, left: Director King Donovan discusses Jayne's taxing cinematic chores with her and a cameraman. The upcoming tub scene is unlike most others in that the soapsuds will evaporate, leaving Jayne cleanly exposed to the camera. Above, right: Director Donovan assures bashful Jayne that it's all in the service of the plot. Below: Jayne, now convinced after much coaxing, finally makes the foamy plunge.

...viously unpublished still, Jayne Mansfield makes it eminently
...this West Texas schoolgirl grew to the stature of a reigning star.

O

Old Age

I don't ever want to grow old. I don't want to become a has-been, an old biddy with scrapbooks of press clippings. Once I start to slip, I'm going to stay home and be a wife and mother full-time.

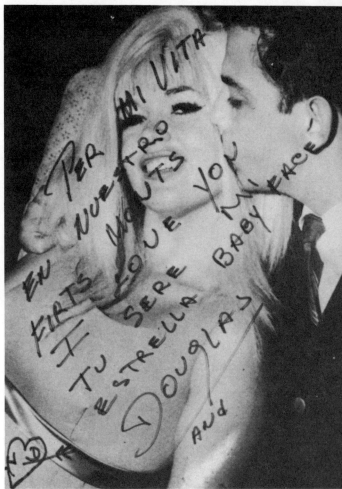

Douglas Olivares

They met in 1960, during Jayne's tour of South America.

He's precious—and so in love. I'm his first love. He won't be 21 for two and a half months yet. So we have to be careful—very careful!

Orgasm

An orgasm with Sam [Brody] is like being in heaven and hell at the same time.

With lawyer and friend Sam Brody. ▶

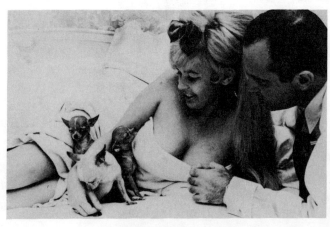

P

Performing for American troops in Korea (1957).

People

I love people. I love it when they love me—recognize me—love me.

Pink

By now I had a gimmick. Pink was my color because
it made me happy. It is bright and gay. "Mansfield
Pink" will become famous, I'd tell anyone who called
it "Mansfield Madness." Now I had something to
intrigue the photographers. Come up for a drink and
paint me pink. I'd invite anyone who had a camera.
I'd add I would be happy to pose for any layouts
they'd like. I was desperate.

Pink Palace 1

Just think of all the publicity I can get with a pink movie star palace! It will not only be a wonderful home, but a good investment in my career. I can dress and act glamorously like a movie star should. I walked my new pet leopard on a leash down Hollywood Boulevard yesterday. I had a big, pink satin bow tied around his neck. And I wore a pink jumpsuit and a big pink picture hat. It was really divine!

Front gate, with the initials JM. ▶

Pink Palace 2

Everyone thinks we have thirty-six bathrooms. I think we can seat twelve.

Pink Palace 3

We have eight bedrooms and thirteen baths. I think we're going to be the cleanest people in the world.

The heart-shaped swimming pool, on the bottom of which was written Mickey's *I love you Jaynie*.

Acrobatics on a private beach with sand imported from Acapulco.

After her Broadway debut, Jayne returned to Hollywood a full-fledged star, prompting PLAYBOY to pose the question, *Will Success Spoil Jayne Mansfield?* She soon quieted any fears, showing no hesitance about peeling down to little more than a winsome smile, as she unabashedly displayed the remarkable Mansfield dimensions for PLAYBOY Magazine and the Playmate Calendar.

as to her place among the film capital's top attractions. But even more impressive than her rapid rise to success was the fact that while other seductive sirens have come and gone, Jayne maintained her firm hold on the imaginations of males everywhere. Like a rare and heady cognac, the voluptuous Mansfield form consistently improved with time. Happily combined with this is Jayne's complete willingness to exhibit her glowing attractions for PLAYBOY at the drop of a lens cap.

The number of starlets willing to pose *deshabillé* in their attempts to obtain recognition has been legion. But once these selfsame lesser lights have attained even a fraction of the status currently enjoyed by Miss Mansfield, they have usually disdained any further display of their charms *au naturel*. To the continuing delight of the PLAYBOY audience, this is not so with Jayne.

For several years, following her initial appearance as the February Playmate, PLAYBOY observed a Valentine tradition of running a current photo story on Jayne. In 1956, she posed for our photographers while columnist Earl Wilson posed the question: *Will Success Spoil Jayne Mansfield?* The answer was a resounding NO! The following year PLAYBOY trekked out to Hollywood to get the facts about *The New Jayne Mansfield.* Once again, Jayne proved that a picture can be worth a thousand words as she uninhibitedly posed before our cameras. Then, in February 1958, PLAYBOY made photographic history. When Jayne appeared completely unadorned in a feature aptly titled *The Nude Jayne Mansfield,* it marked the first occasion of an established star's posing in the altogether for publication.

Playboy 1

They had asked me to pose almost in the nude but not quite that first time and the studio okayed it. I posed in many reclining poses in some leopard leotards. They came out sexy, but the studio press agent and the photographer insisted they were art.

Playboy 2

Playboy offered me big money for another centerfold. I refused. I have never done anything knowingly that would be in bad taste. It just wouldn't match me now as a mother.

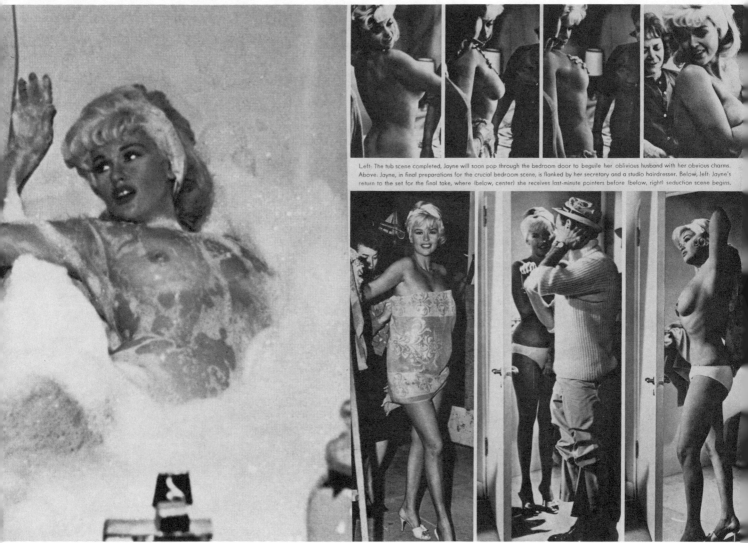

Left: The tub scene completed, Jayne will soon pop through the bedroom door to beguile her oblivious husband with her obvious charms. Above: Jayne, in final preparations for the crucial bedroom scene, is flanked by her secretary and a studio hairdresser. Below, left: Jayne's return to the set for the final take, where (below, center) she receives last-minute pointers before (below, right) seduction scene begins.

Playboy 3

When Tommy Noonan convinced her it would be good publicity for Promises, Promises!, *Jayne finally agreed to let* Playboy *run nude pictures of her—for free!*

I was a bit off, wasn't I? I could have been paid $20,000 for a centerfold.

Playboy was not interested in Jayne's
musical talents.

Pregnancy

Jayne was pregnant during the filming of The Sheriff of Fractured Jaw. *She had quite a lot to do in this movie and she later said:*

My son probably has had more exercise before he was born than he will ever have again.

Jayne, Mickey and Jayne Marie arrive in London to shoot *The Sheriff of Fractured Jaw.*

▲ In *The Sheriff of Fractured Jaw.*

The happy family in 1964: Mickey, his mother, Jayne Marie, Jayne, Miklos, Zoltan and baby Mariska Magdolna. ▶

Promises, Promises!

The film ran briefly in Cleveland, but later the city banned it.

If the judges can't decide, then I feel my opinion is just as good as theirs. They don't know it, but they are really helping me. They are keeping my name before the people. That's all that's important.

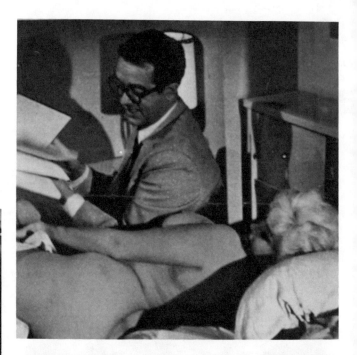

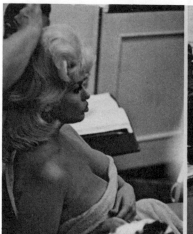

Backstage at the filming of her epidermic epic, *Promises, Promises!*—in which Jayne plays the frustrated passionate wife of a professional gag writer (portrayed by Tommy Noonan) who would rather tickle her risibilities than titillate her sensibilities—Jayne, temporarily clad in a roomy towel (left), prepared to bare all in the opening bubble-bath scene. Right, her entourage makes some final cosmetic touches.

in one scene, her well-distributed proportions hugged by a net costume so sheer that its one function seemed to be the support of a few carefully arranged rhinestones. As might have been expected, the distribution pattern for the film included only a highly limited showing in the United States, in view of our diligent censorship boards. It was left to PLAYBOY to ensure that Jayne's fans would not be deprived of the opportunity to evaluate the merits of her transatlantic performance.

These photos, along with other feats of baring-do on the part of the magnificent Miss Mansfield, were recorded in a February 1960 feature dubbed *The Best of Mansfield*.

Meanwhile, 20th Century-Fox had come to the decision that Jayne's talents as a comedienne should be combined with her love-goddess image to create a film custom-tailored to this individual personality.

The plot of *Promises, Promises!* required Jayne to appear in a bathtub scene, and later in a bedroom *contretemps* with her gag-writer husband (played by long-time comedy actor Tommy Noonan) in which she tries unsuccessfully to arouse his marital interest and take his mind off the constant search for bigger and better punchlines.

To these standard Hollywood ploys,

Jayne applied her natural gifts and histrionic talents, with the end result being first published in PLAYBOY as the highlight of its June 1963 feature, *The Nudest Jayne Mansfield*. Millions of readers of this sellout issue agreed with us that only in Hollywood's land of make-believe could anyone conceive of a plot line wherein Jayne's feminine allure is deliberately ignored by its male target. Unfortunately, the comedic intent of the plot also went unnoticed by that group of latter-day moralists who tried to label the magazine's photo story obscene. This allegation resulted in a trial—and the jury's refusal to agree with the prosecution.

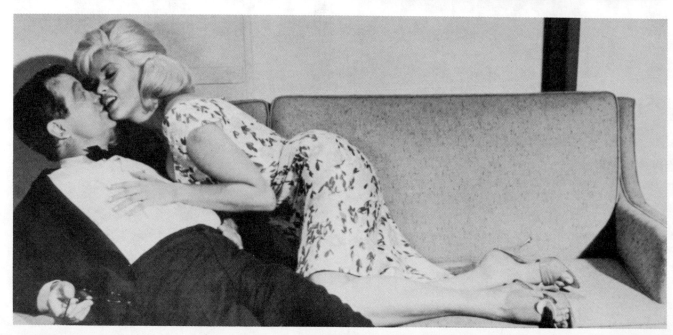

Publicity

Someone mentioned an Eastern pinup establishment that was bootlegging revealing pictures of Jayne. He wondered if she would order an injunction.

Injunction? What do I want with an injunction? Send more pictures immediately! There may be somebody somewhere who doesn't have one! I don't care who they are—men, women, children, grandmothers! We were made for each other!

Punishment

If you're going to do something wrong, do it big
because the punishment is just the same either way.

Roland Maxwell awards Jayne a plaque naming her "Favorite Entertainer" (1960).

Q

Queen

Queen of Refrigeration Week
Queen of Palm Springs Desert Rodeo
Cherry Blossom Queen
Queen Cotton
Nylon Queen
Gas Station Queen
Queen of the Chihauhau Show
Princess of the Freeways
Miss negligee
Miss Tomato
Miss Direct Mail
Miss Lobster
Miss Photoflash
Miss Third Platoon
Miss Orchid
Miss 100% Pure
Miss One For The Road
Miss Blue Bonnet
Miss Electric Switch
Miss Standard Foods
Miss Fire Alarm
Miss July Fourth

In Rome, Jayne is named "Best Actress of the Year" (1962).

A nightclub in the Italian capital awards Jayne a silver Eiffel Tower as its "Most Distinguished Guest" (1962).

Queen Elizabeth II 1

It was the most exciting moment of my life. I was never in awe of any woman before—but I was terribly in awe of her. The Queen has a great inner beauty. I looked at her the way I've seen my fans look at me. I was shivering with ecstasy.

Queen Elizabeth II 2

How beautiful she is. I'm so glad my dress was high in the neck. A queen like Queen Elizabeth deserves that respect.

R

Rape

One night I told my mother I was going to a girl's party. I didn't mention there would be boys there. The kids were all older than I was. I was given a glass of what I thought was lemonade. Actually it was a vodka collins. Drinking was something I always said would never affect me. I wouldn't waste so much time being crocked. I loved life. I wanted to live and not watch it from the sidelines. It was a hot night. I had my third "lemonade" and passed out. The next thing I knew someone was pouring black coffee down me and I was throwing up. We were out on a porch and I was leaning over the banisters. Suddenly I fell unconscious.

One of the boys put me in his car and drove to a parking place so the fresh air blowing into the car would make me come to. I can't remember the details, but I was raped. I couldn't tell my mother. When my period didn't arrive on schedule, my worst fear was

In Sweden during her 1967 European tour, Jayne fought with lawyer/friend Sam Brody.

▼

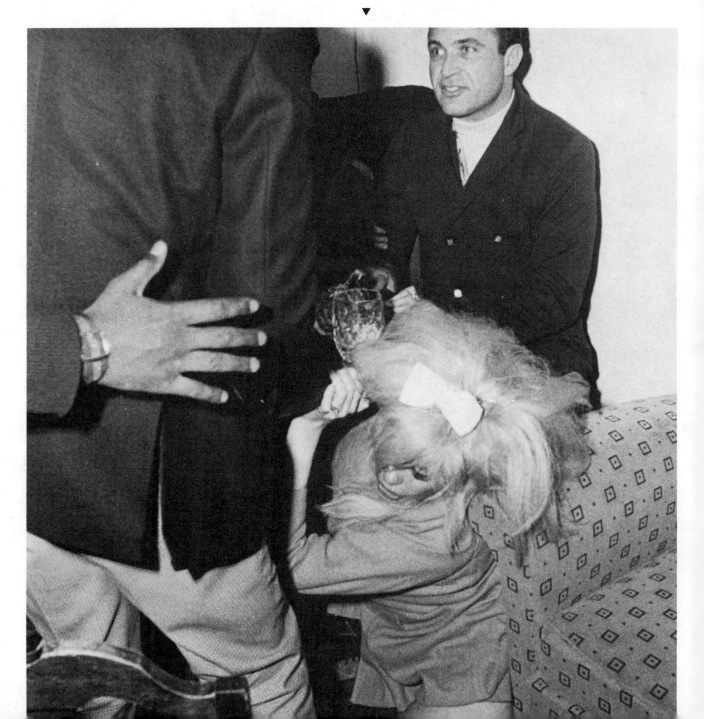

confirmed. I was pregnant! What should I do? Even if I could, I would never have an abortion. To me that is murder! I'd have my baby. But what about Momma? I felt I should get married right away. It wasn't difficult to select a husband at school. Paul J. Mansfield was one of the best-looking students in school.

Records

Shakespeare, Tchaikovsky and Me (MGM, E 4202)

Jayne reads poetry of Shakespeare and others. Selections include: "How Do I Love Thee," "She Walks in Beauty," "Was This That Special Face," and "To the Virgins."

Little Things Mean a Lot

Jayne Busts Up Las Vegas (LP)

An Evening with Jayne Mansfield
with Kurt Jensen and His Orchestra (LP, Hollywood Records, LPH 137)

Heimweh Nach St. Pauli (with Freddy Quinn)
Also available under the title *Freddy et le Nouveau Monde.*

Rome

(1962)

My whole feeling and life has changed. I look at things so differently. It's as though I used to see everything in black and white. Since Rome, I see everything in Technicolor. Now I want to exploit the real me—not just a glamour girl.

▲
◀ At an award ceremony in Rome, a woman knocked Jayne to the ground, screaming, "I'm an actress, too!"

Roquefort

I think the only thing I ever turned down was a chance to be Miss Roquefort Cheese because it didn't sound right.

134

Royalty

I could have been a Princess Grace or Princess Rita. I just couldn't ever marry for titles, unless I happened to love the man who carried them. Marriages for position seldom last. I'd like to have a palace, of course. I may not be a princess, but I am a movie queen, and every queen should have a palace.

Grace Kelly ▲

S

Nelson Sardelli

We had a beautiful romance. He is young and virile and sexy and wild in bed, in life. I thought we had a real thing going--and then I heard that he was married.

Sex Appeal

It's all in the mind. It's what you have inside—the feelings that you transmit—that counts! The rest is all tinsel. Sex appeal has nothing to do with body proportions.

Sex 1

I love sex.

Sex 2

I believe that sex is the most important human factor between two people. I believe that in physical relationships everything goes. The wildest form of love is beautiful. It should be tender. It should be brutal, sadistic. It should, at times, even be masochistic.

Sex 3

In Las Vegas for a performance at the Dunes Hotel, Jayne spent a night in bed with two men, one a ballet dancer and the other a producer. The producer's wife caught them in the act, sued her husband for divorce and was awarded $100,000 by the court.

What other movie actress is worth $100,000 for a single night in bed?

Sex Goddess

I've outgrown all of that sex goddess stuff. No one was taking me seriously, and I have to prove that I am serious. And to think I worked so hard to join the ranks of Brigitte Bardot, Marilyn Monroe and Jane Russell.

Shakespeare

I can think of no greater beauty than the reading of a Shakespeare sonnet with a background of Tchaikovsky's romantic and beautifully poetic music. It is like a great Broadway musical.

Star

I didn't come to Hollywood to be the girl next door. I came to be a movie star.

Marilyn Monroe ▼

Striptease

On her striptease act in Las Vegas:

I know the experts say a girl can be just as sexy in high-necked dresses, but that's the hard way. If handled tastefully cleavage seldom fails. It's the easiest way to get eyes focused on the right places.

In this strip I do, I have a perfect chance to attract men's eyes, so I want to be just right. It's a challenge.

▲ Striptease in *Primitive Love*.

Success

I am not conceited. I don't really think I am the most beautiful woman in the world at all. If I can create some illusion to that effect, and it seems I have, then that is what spells success for me.

François Chalais greets Jayne at the Nice airport.

Supermarkets

When asked why she made so many appearances at supermarkets:

I do it for the money, I get five thousand dollars in cash and five thousand dollars in merchandise.

Parade during the Cannes Film Festival (1958).

T

Elizabeth Taylor

Elizabeth Taylor and I are unique in the fact that we believe in old-fashioned marriage. And children with marriage—that love and marriage come together. We are both, foremost, good mothers and family women, as strange as that may sound. But it is a fact. Elizabeth and I have generous curves, and we both share a problem keeping them.

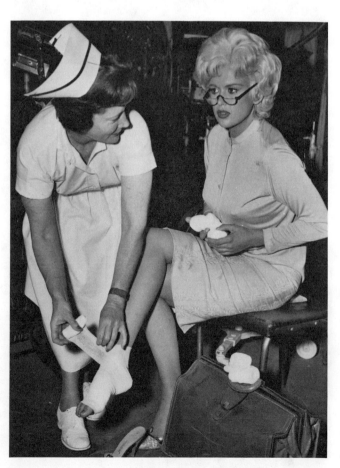

◀ Jayne injured her foot while filming her television debut (1962).

Television

The Bachelor

Musical comedy.

Follow the Sun

Episode: "The Dumbest Blonde."
Director: Robert Butler.
With Barry Coe, Jayne Mansfield and Brian Keith.
Black-and-white, 54 minutes, broadcast on 2/4/62.

The Alfred Hitchcock Hour

Episode: "Hangover."
Director: Bernard Girard.
With Tony Randall, Jayne Mansfield and Dody Heath.
B/W, 52 minutes, broadcast on 12/6/62.

The Jack Benny Show

Sketch with Benny, Mansfield, Don Wilson and Dennis Day. (Benny did the identical sketch with Marilyn Monroe 10 years earlier, in September 1953.) Broadcast on 11/26/63.

Burke's Law

Episode: "Who Killed Molly?"
Director: Don Weis.
With Gene Barry, Gary Conway, Hoagy Carmichael and Jayne Mansfield.
B/W, 52 minutes, broadcast on 3/27/64.

The Jayne Mansfield Hour

Director: Mervin Nelson.
With Jayne Mansfield, Matt Cimber, Eric Rhodes, Ronnie Cunningham and Craig Timberlake.
B/W, 30 minutes.
This pilot episode featured Jayne as Jayne Marlowe, a character based on Rita Marlowe. NBC decided against turning it into a series.

Elizabeth Taylor ▶

Shirley Temple

I was always dancing to the radio and play-acting. I wasn't quite sure what I wanted to be. Sometimes I thought I'd become another Shirley Temple! I loved her. Later I played that I was like Lana Turner. I like the sexy sweet way she looked. In Hollywood, I was accused of trying to imitate Marilyn Monroe. Actually I was completely different. But Jackie Kennedy imitated my voice on TV when she was in the White House.

Theater

George Axelrod
Will Success Spoil Rock Hunter?
(premiere October 13, 1955, at the Belasco Theater,
New York)
Director: George Axelrod
Rita Marlowe   Jayne Mansfield
Masseur   Lew Gallo
George MacCauley   Orson Bean
Michael Freeman   Walter Matthau
Irving LaSalle   Martin Gabel
Harry Kaye   Harry Clark
Secretary   Carol Grace
Bronk Brannigan   William Thourlby
Bellman   David Sheiner
Chauffeur   Michael Tolan

William Inge
Bus Stop
(premiere May 16, 1964, at Yonkers Playhouse,
Yonkers, New York)
Director: Matt Cimber
Cherie   Jayne Mansfield
Cowboy   Stephen Brooks
Bus Driver   Mickey Hargitay
with Ann B. Davis, Rob Jackson and Elizabeth
Hartman

Anita Loos & Joseph Fields
Gentlemen Prefer Blondes
(premiere 1964 in Framingham, Mass.)
with Jayne Mansfield as *Lorelei*

Champagne Complex
(premiere 1964 in Milwaukee, Minn.)
Director: Matt Cimber
with Jayne Mansfield and Matt Cimber

The Rabbit Habit
(premiere December 1, 1965)
Director: Matt Cimber
with Jayne Mansfield

With Ann B. Davis, Elizabeth Hartman and Stephen Brooks on the
▼ set of *Bus Stop.*

U

Underwater

Jayne's first step on the road to fame took place during a promotional tour for Jane Russell's Underwater. *The day before Russell's arrival in Florida, Jayne was photographed in a bikini, then dove into a swimming pool.*

I dived in, undid my bikini top, and came up bouncing. I planned it differently. I was going to come up and toss the bikini top to the photographers. Because it wasn't my size, I had trouble getting it over my head. I thought I'd blown the whole thing.

Far from blowing the whole thing, Jayne made the stunt immensely successful. The wire services carried Jayne Mansfield's name and picture around the world. Headlines sizzled: "Jayne Outpoints Jane."

Mae West

Mae West held a press conference at which she expected Mickey to state that his association with Jayne was for publicity reasons only. Instead, Mickey said that he was in love with Jayne and that they wanted to get married.

Mae's bodyguard immediately launched an attack and knocked Hargitay to the ground. In the ensuing fight Mae also went down. "They can't do this to me," she shouted. "I'm an institution." After the row much animosity was exchanged. Mae called Mickey, "Mr. Universe, last year's model,". making Mickey wonder;. "If I'm an old model, what does that make her!" But Jayne poured oil on troubled waters:

I've always been told to respect people older than myself. She's 64 and if I look that good when I'm 64, nothing will bother me. To me she's a great entertainer.

Women

I need a man around. I have to sleep with a man every night. I really do. It has to be a man. Girls just don't turn me on—sometimes I wish they did. It would be easier.

World Peace

A reporter once asked me if I would do a striptease for Chroetsjow—until I was completely naked—if this would lead to world peace.

"Of course," I said, "and many other things too."

With George Harrison (left) and John Lennon in Hollywood ▼ (August 26, 1964).

Wrinkles

Wrinkles frighten me. I can't face old age. No glamour girl can face old age. Marilyn Monroe couldn't face it.

Y

The Y in Jayne:

Because of displayed and extreme elusiveness it was given to me after a Yale party.

Youth

I looked at that kid in the mirror, a kid with brownish hair and braces, and I swore that one fine day I would become a movie star. A real star!

▼ At 16 years.

▲ At 3 years.

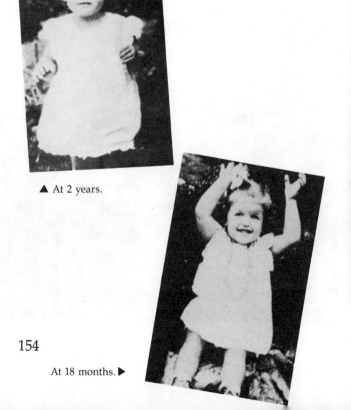

▲ At 2 years.

At 18 months. ▶

The crew of the American aircraft carrier *Tarawa* provided an original greeting when Jayne visited the ship in Rotterdam harbor (October 11, 1957).

June 29, 1967

"One misty morning Jayne Mansfield hit a stationary
truck at full speed and was decapitated."—Jan Cremer
in *Logboek*.

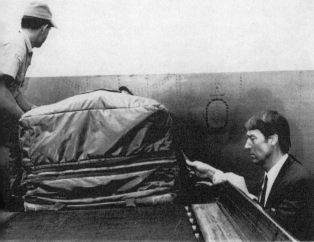

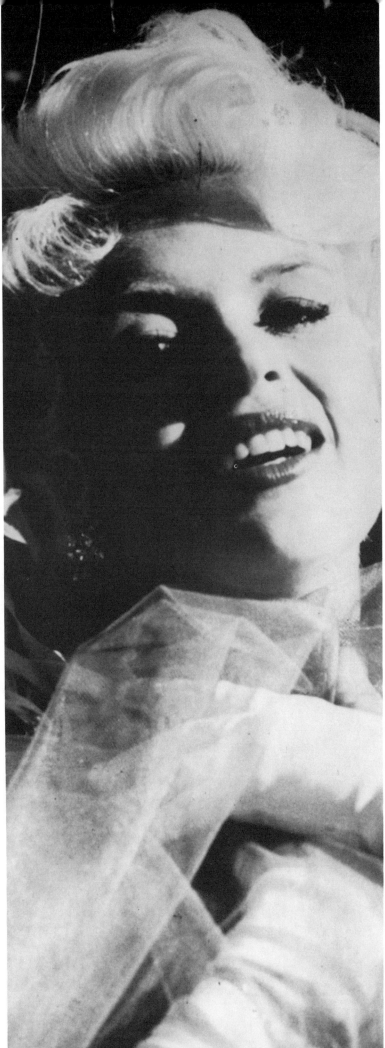

19 April	**1933**	Jayne Palmer is born at Bryn Mawr Hospital, Bryn Mawr, Pennsylvania.
	1945	Jayne gets her first dancing lessons at "Mrs Louise Finley's dance classes."
28 January	**1950**	Marriage to Paul Mansfield.
8 November	**1950**	Jayne Marie Mansfield is born.
	1954	Jayne debutes in *Female Jungle*.
February	**1955**	Jayne appears as Playmate in *Playboy*.
8 January	**1958**	Divorce from Paul Mansfield.
13 January	**1958**	Marriage to Mickey Hargitay.
	1959	Jayne is introduced to Queen Elizabeth II.
11 June	**1962**	Mickey Hargitay leaves Jayne Mansfield.

26 May	**1964**	Jayne plays the leading role in William Inge's Bus Stop, which is under the direction of Matt Cimber.
30 September	**1964**	Marriage to Matt Cimber.
29 June	**1967**	While driving her car in the mist on the highway between Slidell and New Orleans, Jayne hits a stationary truck at 80 m.p.h. and is instantly killed. Sam Brody, Ronnie Harrison and three of her children, who are also in the car, survive the accident.

▼ Jayne Marie in *Playboy*: like mother, like daughter.

The Citadel Press Film Series

From Federico Fellini to Moe Howard and the Three Stooges, Woody Allen to John Wayne, the Citadel Press Film Series is America's largest film book library. Now with more than 100 titles in print, books in the series make perfect gifts--for a loved one, a friend, or yourself!

The Films of...

Alan Ladd
Alfred Hitchcock
All Talking! All Singing!
  All Dancing!
Anthony Quinn
The Bad Guys
Barbara Stanwyck
Barbra Streisand:
  The First Decade
Barbra Streisand:
  The Second Decade
Bela Lugosi
Bette Davis
Bing Crosby
Boris Karloff
Bowery Boys
Brigitte Bardot
Burt Reynolds
Carole Lombard
Cary Grant
Cecil B. DeMille
Character People
Charles Bronson
Charlie Chaplin
Charlton Heston
Chevalier
Clark Gable
Classics of the Gangster
  Film
Classics of the Horror Film
Classics of the Silent Screen
Cliffhanger
Clint Eastwood
Curly: Biography of a
  Superstooge
David Niven
Detective in Film
Dick Tracy
Doris Day
Dustin Hoffman

Elizabeth Taylor
Elvis Presley
Errol Flynn
Federico Fellini
The Fifties
The Forties
Forgotten Films to Remember
Frank Sinatra
Fredric March
Fritz Lang
Gary Cooper
Gene Kelley
Ginger Rogers
Gloria Swanson
Great Adventure Films
Great British Films
Great French Films
Great German Films
Great Romantic Films
Great Spy Films
Gregory Peck
Greta Garbo
Harry Warren and the
  Hollywood Musical
Hedy Lamarr
Henry Fonda
Hollywood Cheesecake:
  60 Years of Leg Art
Hollywood's Hollywood
Howard Hughes in Hollywood
Humphrey Bogart
Ingrid Bergman
Jack Lemmon
Jack Nicholson
James Cagney
James Mason
Jane Fonda
Jeanette MacDonald and
  Nelson Eddy
Jean Harlow

Jewish Image in American
  Film
Joan Crawford
John Garfield
John Huston
John Wayne
John Wayne Reference
  Book
Judy Garland
Katharine Hepburn
Kirk Douglas
Lana Turner
Laurel and Hardy
Lauren Bacall
Laurence Olivier
Love in the Film
Mae West
Marilyn Monroe
Marlene Dietrich
Marlon Brando
Moe Howard and the
  Three Stooges
Montgomery Clift
More Character People
More Classics of the
  Horror Film
Myrna Loy
Non-Western Films of
  John Ford
Norma Shearer
Olivia de Havilland
Paul Newman
Peter Lorre
Pictorial History of Science
  Fiction Films
Pictorial History of Sex
  in Films
Pictorial History of War
  Films

Pictorial History of the
  Western Film
Rebels: The Rebel Hero
  in Films
Rita Hayworth
Robert Redford
Robert Taylor
Ronald Colman
Ronald Reagan
The Seventies
Sex in the Movies
Sci-Fi 2
Sherlock Holmes
Shirley MacLaine
Shirley Temple
The Sixties
Sophia Loren
Spencer Tracy
Steve McQueen
Susan Hayward
Tarzan of the Movies
They Had Faces Then
The Thirties
Those Glorious Glamour Years
Three Stooges Book of Scripts
Three Stooges Book of Scripts,
  Vol. 2
The Twenties
20th Century Fox
Tyrone Power
Warren Beatty
W.C. Fields
Western Films of John Ford
William Holden
William Powell
Woody Allen
World War II

Ask for these titles at your bookseller. And send for our listing with prices: Citadel Press, 120 Enterprise Avenue, Secaucus, New Jersey 07094.